TROPICAL RAIN FOREST

APRIL PULLEY SAYRE

TWENTY-FIRST CENTURY BOOKS

Brookfield, Connecticut

For Dr. Patricia Chapple Wright, my mentor in the Forest.
~A. P. S.~

ACKNOWLEDGMENTS

A special thanks to the scientists who reviewed all or part of the manu-
script: Dr. Larry E. DeBuhr, Director of Education, Missouri Botanical
Garden; and Dr. Donald Stone, Director, Organization for Tropical
Studies.

Twenty-First Century Books
A Division of The Millbrook Press, Inc.
2 Old New Milford Road
Brookfield, Connecticut 06804

Library of Congress Cataloging-in-Publication Data
Sayre, April Pulley.
Tropical rain forest/April Pulley Sayre.—1st ed.
p. cm. — (Exploring earth's biomes)
Includes index.
1. Rain forest ecology—Juvenile literature. 2. Rain forests—Juvenile
literature. [1. Rain forest ecology. 2. Rain forests. 3. Ecology.]
I. Title. II. Series: Sayre, April Pulley. Exploring earth's biomes.
QH541.5.R27S28 1994   574.5′2642—dc20
                                                            94–25427
ISBN 0-8050-2826-9
First Edition—1994

Printed in the United States of America
All first editions are printed on acid-free paper ∞.

10   9   8   7   6

Photo Credits
p. 8: Alan D. Carey/Photo Researchers, Inc.; pp. 15, 25 (inset): Bill and
Diane Lowrie/Photo Researchers, Inc.; pp. 19, 36: Frans Lanting/Minden
Pictures; p. 22: Bruce Iversen, Science Photo Library/ Photo Researchers,
Inc.; p. 25: G. I. Bernard/Earth Scenes; p. 28: Mark Moffett/Minden
Pictures; p. 29: Gunter Ziesler/Peter Arnold, Inc.; p. 30: Hans and Judy
Beste/Animals Animals; p. 33: Paul Freed/Animals Animals; p. 35:
Kenneth T. Nemuras; p. 37: Tom McHugh/Photo Researchers, Inc.; p. 49:
Scott Wallace/Sipa Press; p. 55: April Pulley Sayre.

CONTENTS

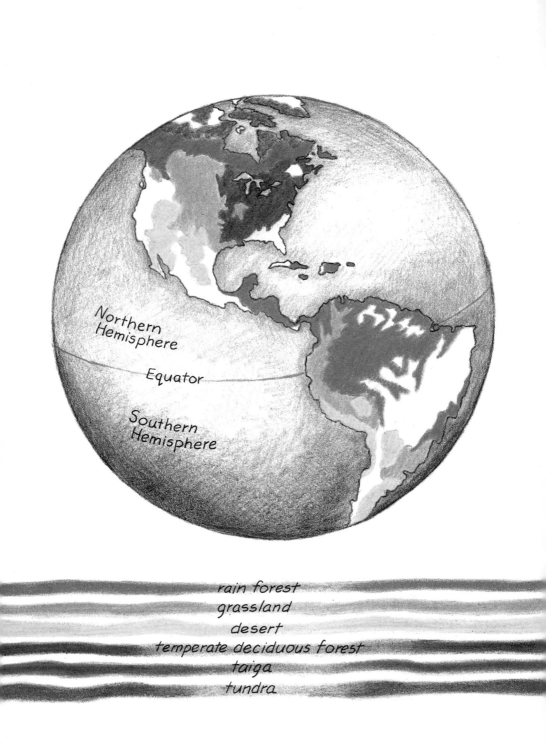

Northern
Hemisphere

Equator

Southern
Hemisphere

rain forest
grassland
desert
temperate deciduous forest
taiga
tundra

INTRODUCTION

Take a look at the earth as a whole and you'll see its surface can be divided into living communities called biomes. Desert, rain forest, tundra, taiga, temperate deciduous forest, grassland, and polar desert are some of the main terrestrial biomes—biomes on land. Each biome has particular kinds of plants and animals living in it. Scientists also identify other biomes not mentioned here, including aquatic biomes—biomes of lakes, streams, and the sea.

When their boundaries are drawn on a globe, terrestrial biomes look like horizontal bands stacked up from Pole to Pole. Starting from the equator and moving outward toward the Poles, you'll find rain forests, grasslands, deserts, and grasslands once again. Then things change a little. The next biomes we think of—temperate deciduous forests, taiga, and tundra—exist only in the Northern Hemisphere. Why is this true? Well, if you look in the Southern Hemisphere, you'll see there's very little land in the regions where these biomes would supposedly lie. There's simply nowhere for these biomes to exist! Conditions on small pieces of land—islands and peninsulas—that lie in these areas are greatly affected by sea conditions and are very different from those on continents.

But why do biomes generally develop in these bands? The answer lies in the earth's climate and geology. Climate is affected by the angle at which sunlight hits the earth. At the equator, sunlight passes through the atmosphere and hits the earth straight on, giving it its full energy. At the Poles, sunlight must pass through more atmosphere and it hits the earth at an angle, with less energy per square foot. Other factors also influence where biomes lie: the bands of rising and falling air that circulate around the planet; the complex weather systems created by jutting mountains, deep valleys, and cold currents; the glaciers that have scoured the lands in years past; and the activities of humans. This makes biome boundaries less regular than the simplified bands described above.

❦ 1 ❦
THE TROPICAL
RAIN FOREST BIOME

Steamy, hot, dense jungle is what many people think of when they hear the phrase *tropical rain forest.* They imagine Tarzan swinging from vines and explorers using machetes to slowly hack their way through tangled undergrowth. But don't believe everything you see in the movies. In reality, a mature, uncut rain forest is quite easy to walk through. High in the air a canopy of treetops blocks the sunlight, so few plants grow on the forest floor between the trees. It's only in light-filled areas, near rivers and roadsides, in forest gaps, and in partially logged forests, where you'll find dense green "jungly" undergrowth.

Tropical rain forests are wet—really wet. One year the rain forest in Cherrapunji, India, got 1,042 inches (2,647 centimeters) of rain. That's more than 20 times as much rain as New York City gets in an average year! These wet forests are home to an amazing number of animal and plant species—from howler monkeys to tapirs, to lemurs, giant butterflies, and boa constrictors. In fact, tropical rain forests contain almost half of the plant and animal species on earth. That's pretty amazing considering tropical rain forests cover only about 7 percent of the earth's land surface.

Like desert or tundra, the tropical rain forest is a biome—a geographic area that has a certain kind of climate and a certain community of plants and animals. Stretching in a broken band centered around the equator, tropical rain

*Tropical rain forests have high canopies
that block sunlight from the plants below.*

forests are located in more than 40 countries. But many of these countries contain only small remnants of tropical forest. The three largest blocks of tropical rain forest are located in Central and West Africa, mainly in Zaire; Southeast Asia, mostly in Indonesia; and the Neotropics, primarily in Brazil.

There's also another kind of rain forest not covered in this book. Temperate rain forests, such as the forest in Olympic National Park in Washington State, get a lot of rain. But they are generally cooler, contain fewer species, and have a different structure than tropical rain forests. And of course they're located in the temperate zone of the earth, *not* the tropics.

TYPES

There are many different types of tropical rain forests. Two main types are:

• **Cloud forests**   These forests are found at middle to high elevations on mountains. Mist, clouds, and rain keep these forests wet. Thick growths of mosses, ferns, and other plants live on the branches of the trees, which are denser and shorter than those in lowland forests.

• **Lowland forests**   These forests are found at low elevations. They have tall trees with less growth on their branches than do cloud-forest trees. Moisture comes primarily from intermittent rain, not from the constant cloud cover found in cloud forests.

TEMPERATURES

• Air temperature changes little during the day or during the year.
• Average yearly temperature is at least 75°F (24°C) but can be as high as 86°F (30°C), depending on the forest's altitude. (At higher altitudes, temperatures are cooler.)

WEATHER

• Average relative humidity is high: 77 percent to 88 percent.
• Rain forests farther away from the equator experience more marked dry seasons and wet seasons.
• Storms may be strong.
• Rain forests average 80 or more inches (200 centimeters) of rain a year.

SOIL

• Tropical rain forest soils vary, but they are generally nutrient poor. The topsoil layer is thin—often not more than an inch (2.5 centimeters) deep.

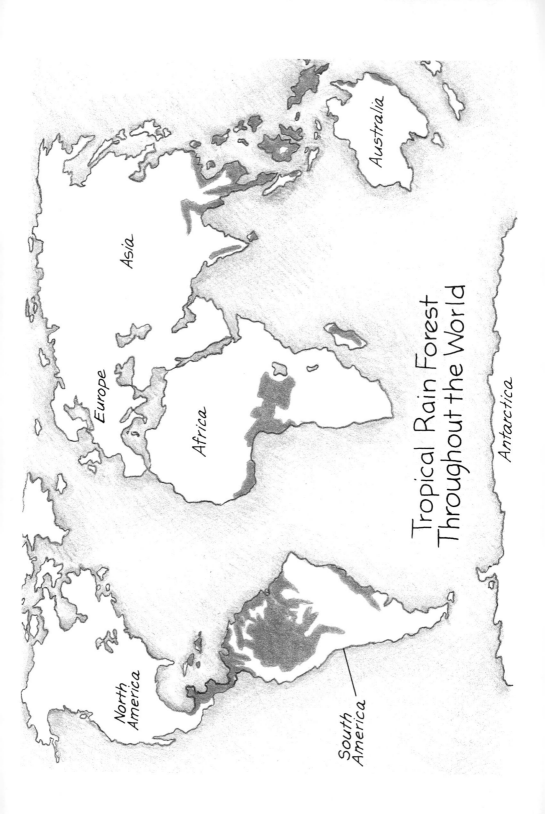

Tropical Rain Forest
Throughout the World

Australia

Asia

Europe

Africa

Antarctica

North
America

South
America

- There is very little decaying leaf matter on the forest floor.
- The rain forest's nutrients are held in the trees, not the soil. After the rain forest is cut and burned, the soil is good for farming for only a few years.

PLANTS

- Plant biomass—the total weight of plant matter—for a given area is generally higher than in other biomes.
- Plants are arranged in a complex, layered forest structure from emergents to canopy to the understory to the forest floor.
- Many species of trees, vines, and epiphytes, lots of woody plants, very little underbrush.

ANIMALS

- Abundant wildlife; very high species diversity.
- Insects, and arboreal (tree-dwelling) mammals, such as monkeys, abound.
- Many animals are specialized to feed on just one or two foods. They have complex relationships with other animals and plants.

2
RAIN FORESTS OF
THE NEOTROPICS

If you're looking for giant otters, algae-covered sloths, prowling jaguars, or poison dart frogs, look no farther than the Neotropics. The Neotropics is a geographic region encompassing Central America, the northern portion of South America, and the West Indies. The rain forests of this region stretch from northern Mexico to Brazil, and along the Atlantic and North Pacific coasts of South America. Small patches also exist in Puerto Rico, Trinidad, Cuba, and other islands. (Hawaii contains tropical rain forest but is not located in the Neotropics.)

Within the Neotropics lies the largest tract of tropical rain forest in the world: the Amazon rain forest. You can string up a hammock on a boat out of São Paolo, Brazil, and spend weeks traveling thousands of miles deeper into this forest. But truly exploring this place will take not weeks, but a lifetime, because the Amazon rain forest is immense. It stretches more than 2.3 million square miles (6 million square kilometers). Nearly 60 percent of it lies in Brazil. But the rest of it spreads out over eight countries and territories: Venezuela, Colombia, Peru, Bolivia, Ecuador, Guyana, Suriname, and French Guiana.

Neotropical rain forests are rich in resources, with grandeur sometimes on an almost unimaginable scale. Here are just a few amazing facts about these forests and their inhabitants:

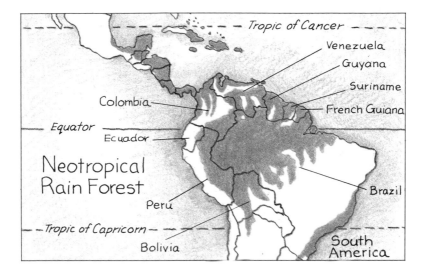

- Some 1,600 species of the pineapple family exist in South America. Many are bromeliads, meaning they grow high on trees.
- The Chocó forest in Colombia is estimated to contain 8,000 to 9,000 different plant species and more than 100 birds unique to that area.
- The small country of Ecuador has more than twice as many plant species as the entire continental United States.
- The Amazon River is so big that 20 percent of the earth's freshwater runs through it each day.

Not only are the plants and animals of Neotropical forests remarkable, the people are, too. Hundreds of different cultures and languages have developed in these forests, and over thousands of years, many rain forest people have built up a storehouse of valuable knowledge. Also, as you'll find out in the rest of this book, the Neotropical rain forests affect not just rain forest residents, but the lives of people worldwide. These forests play a critical role in the world's climate and are a source of fruits, nuts, vegetables, minerals, wood, lifesaving medicines, and other products.

3
RAIN FOREST
WEATHER, CLIMATE,
AND GEOLOGY

Weather forecasters have an easier job in the tropics than they do in temperate regions. Day after day there's little change in the tropical weather. As scientists Ken Miyata and Adrian Forsyth wrote, "They [the tropical forecasters] could probably tape their forecast twice a year, once during the wet season and once during the dry season. . . ." Their forecasts would be right most of the time.

This steady, mostly predictable weather isn't important just to farmers in Malaysia, fishermen in Costa Rica, or beachgoers in Rio. It makes rain forests possible, and it affects the entire earth. Tropical rain forests play a crucial role in the world's weather patterns and climate—in the formation of rain, the worldwide transfer of heat, and the global balance of greenhouse gases.

RAIN FOREST WEATHER

Rain forests tend to get rain—and lots of it. Over 80 inches (200 centimeters) per year is the average. Some places, such as the Colombian Chocó, average more than 360 inches (914 centimeters) of rain per year! Although cloud forests don't get much rain at certain times of the year, their cloak of clouds keeps these forests moist.

'Tis Not the Season Tropical rain forests are located in a belt called the tropics, which stretches from the Tropic of

Cloud forests receive little rain, but clouds and mist keep them wet year-round.

Capricorn south of the equator to the Tropic of Cancer north of the equator. Unlike other parts of the earth, the tropics are about the same distance from the sun all year long. As a result, days are the same length. The sun rises and sets at about the same time every day. The average temperature is fairly constant year-round, too—in the Amazon basin it may be 82.2°F (27.9°C) in the dry season, dropping only to 78.5°F (25.8°C) in the cloudy, wet season. The tropics don't experience a spring, summer, fall, and winter as other parts of the earth do.

Heated Air and Wet Winds   For the most part, tropical rain forests are located where concentrated sunlight heats air, which, as it rises, cools and drops rain. But a few rain forests extend northward or southward beyond the tropics, in areas where a tropiclike climate occurs. These conditions are formed where trade winds blow across warm ocean currents and bring moisture to the land. These areas include northeastern India, southeastern Madagascar, southeastern Brazil, northeastern Australia, and southeastern China.

Wet *and* **Dry**   Some rain forests experience wet seasons and dry seasons. The tropical areas farthest from the equator experience one or two rainy seasons and one or two dry seasons each year. During these dry seasons, some tree species shed their leaves. Other trees keep their leaves all year, and still others shed their leaves at times unrelated to wetness or dryness. Rain forests closer to the equator tend to have rain all year long, and experience little or no wet or dry season.

The Humidity Blanket   Tropical rain forests may be steamy, but they don't usually get super hot, like deserts. Insulated by a blanket of humid air, tropical rain forests warm up and cool off slowly. During the day, the average 80 percent humidity keeps much of the sun's energy from reaching the ground. But at night this humid air helps hold the heat close to the ground, keeping the forest warm. As a result, tropical rain forests don't cool off as quickly at night as do deserts, which have very low humidity.

High *and* **Low**   Rain forests at low altitudes tend to have warm, even temperatures. But at higher elevations, rain forests, especially cloud forests, can be much colder. For each 1,000 feet (300 meters) you go up a mountain, the temperature drops about 3°F (1.7°C). In rare instances, temperatures can drop below freezing in mountain rain forests.

A GLOBAL WEATHER MACHINE
Each year millions of acres of tropical rain forest are destroyed. Many scientists are worried about this destruc-

tion because there are important links between these vast forests and the world's weather patterns and climate.

Water for the Forest Half the rain in the Amazon forest is brought by winds from the Atlantic Ocean. The other half comes from the forest itself. It evaporates from the plants in the rain forest's canopy when the hot tropical sun heats it. This hot, moist air rises from the forest and cools, forming clouds and rain. In this way, the rain forest is actually responsible for much of its own water.

Rain, Rain, Don't Go Away If a large portion of the Amazon rain forest is cut down, the water cycle will be disrupted. Already, in some places where most of the forest has been cut but patches remain, no rain falls on the areas without forest, while black clouds hang over the rain forest patches and rain all day. Overall, scientists predict that the water formerly held and cycled by the forest will be lost to the atmosphere when the forest is cut. Scientists predict that large-scale deforestation will change weather patterns so that less of the Atlantic Ocean's water will arrive over the Amazon. As a result, the Amazon will become permanently, drastically drier. This is one of the reasons scientists believe that once much of the Amazon rain forest is cut, it cannot renew itself.

The Global Heat Pump Rain forests near the equator play an important role in a global heat pump—a complex global air and energy exchange system. At the equator, the sun's rays pass through the atmosphere and hit the earth directly or nearly directly, so their energy is concentrated in a small area. As a result, the tropics receive more of the sun's energy than the rest of the earth. The evapotranspiration of water over the rain forest captures some of this heat and releases it

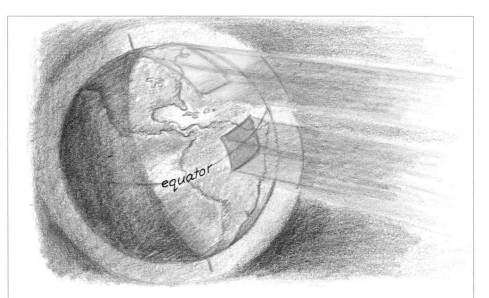

At the equator, the sun's rays hit the earth directly and their energy is concentrated in a small area. Farther away from the equator, the sun's rays hit the earth at an angle. Their energy spreads over a large area.

slowly. This creates winds and air currents that pass along the warmth to other parts of the earth.

Hold Back the Floods   Vast green expanses of rain forest help absorb and slow down torrential tropical rains. In deforested areas, rain washes away what soil is left into rivers. The soil flows into estuaries, clogging them and killing many aquatic plants and animals. Because estuaries and bays are nurseries for young fish, crabs, and shrimp, this damage can seriously hurt the fishing industry.

A PART OF MANY CYCLES

The water cycle discussed above is only one of the many natural cycles at work on our planet. Carbon, sulfur, nitrogen, and other elements are used and reused, lost and

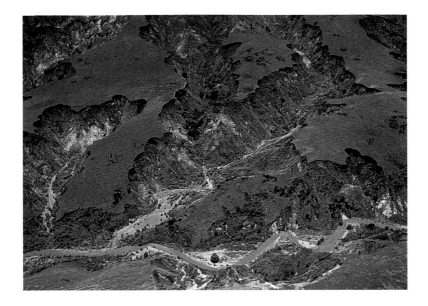

*Precious red soil washes off
deforested hills into the river below.*

recovered, by plants, animals, fungi, and microbes all over the world. Rain forests, with their storehouse of organisms, play an important part in these global cycles. Consider these facts, for instance:

Greenhouse Gases   These gases act like the glass panes of a greenhouse, allowing sunlight into the earth's atmosphere, but only allowing some of the sunlight-generated heat to escape. Greenhouse gases keep the earth warm, but lately their quantity has increased sharply and scientists expect them to cause unfavorable changes in the global climate. When rain forest is burned, carbon dioxide and other greenhouse gases are released. An estimated 25 percent of the human-caused greenhouse gases released on earth are from the burning of tropical forests. Rain forest destruction contributes to the buildup of greenhouse gases that is

EVAPOTRANSPIRATION DEMONSTRATION

Leaves leak. They lose water through their cell walls and through tiny holes called stomates, which they also use to pull in carbon dioxide and get rid of oxygen. The process by which water is lost through a plant's leaves is called transpiration. When this "lost" water evaporates over the forest, the process is called evapotranspiration. In the Amazon, this water from evapotranspiration eventually forms clouds that rain back down onto the forest.

To see evapotranspiration at work, tie a clear plastic bag around the leafy end of a tree branch in a sunny place. Secure the bag with a twist-tie. Wait an hour, then come back and look at the bag. Do you see droplets of water condensed on the inside of the bag? That water evapotranspired from the tree's leaves. Try the bag test on several different kinds of plants—cacti, leafy trees, shrubs, or whatever plants are available. See which ones seem to give off more water. Does the time of day or type of weather make a difference?

changing our earth's climate, possibly leading to consequences such as rising sea levels, warmer global temperatures, altered weather patterns, and extinction of species that cannot tolerate the new conditions.

Carbon Dioxide   Because plants take in carbon dioxide when they carry out photosynthesis, some scientists hope the existing rain forest can absorb part of the extra carbon dioxide released by factories, cars, and other modern sources. In this way, the greenhouse effect might be slowed. But it is unknown if this will really work.

Oxygen   For a long time, scientists thought that rain forests were the "lungs" of the planet. They believed rain forest plants created much of the earth's oxygen. But new evidence has changed that view. Scientists now believe that the decay of rain forest plants uses up about as much oxygen as the living plants release. Obviously, scientists still have a lot to learn about the complexities of global climate.

The Big Picture   Even though scientists haven't figured out the whole picture yet, they do know that rain forests play an important role in the global climate. Many scientists worry that tinkering with this global climate by cutting down the rain forest is a dangerous experiment. The consequences may be dire. And because we've only one earth to work with, we'll have to live with whatever results we get.

SOIL: THE FOUNDATION OF LIFE

Rain forests might look green and lush, but the soils they grow upon are often nutrient poor and not good for farming. A tropical rain forest may have only 1 or 2 inches (2.5 or 5 centimeters) of topsoil, while a temperate deciduous forest can have 7 inches (18 centimeters) or more. The key to the rain forest's lush appearance is that its nutrients are held in its plants, then quickly decomposed and reused. Very little becomes part of the soil. That's why removing trees from the rain forest steals away the "nutrient wealth" of the forest. What's left is soil that's usually infertile, and can only support farming for a few years. These soils are very different from those in temperate deciduous forests, where most nutrients are held in the soil.

Old Soils   Part of the reason rain forest soils are poor is because they're ancient. Many are more than 100 million years old, making them some of the oldest soils on earth. Over the years, rain has leached, or washed away, minerals from these soils, leaving them acidic and less fertile. Sunshine bakes some tropical soils into a hard, red clay. Other soils can't hold dissolved nutrients very well, or turn

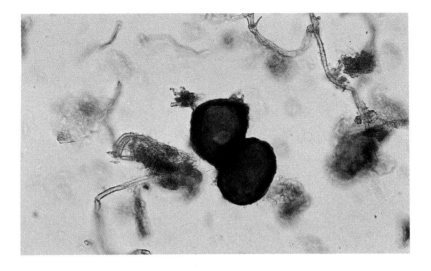

Fossilized pollen grains hold clues to plant life of the past.

minerals that plants need into unusable compounds. Only about 6 percent of the Amazon's soils are actually fertile and good for agriculture. These fertile lands are mixed up in a patchwork of poor soils underneath the vast rain forest.

ANCIENT ISLANDS OF LIFE

Believe it or not, rain forest plant species once grew in Tennessee, in Alaska, and in London, England. Palm trees even grew in Greenland! Fossilized pollen grains prove it. Over millions of years, rain forests have spread during warmer, wetter times, and contracted during drier, colder times. They have also shifted as continents changed position on the globe. Today, scientists have identified patches of rain forest where there are many more species than in other areas. Presumably, these are rain forest refugia— islands of rain forest that survived even when the climate was dry and cold. Some plants and animals in temperate forests, deserts, and other land biomes may have evolved from these ancient rain forest survivors.

4
RAIN FOREST
PLANTS

In the year-round warmth and wetness of the tropics, you might expect plants to grow tall and lush. Tropical rain forest plants do. Trees reach heights of 250 feet (76 meters). A single rafflesia flower can weigh a whopping 38 pounds (17.2 kilograms)! And in just 24 hours, a bamboo plant can grow a yard (almost a meter) taller.

Despite the warmth and abundant rainfall of the region, tropical rain forest plants face their share of challenges. Chief among these is nutrient scarcity. Tropical rain forest plants compete with one another for scarce nutrients, and also for light and space to grow. In addition, many plants have had to develop defenses against a host of hungry plant eaters.

WHAT'S SO SPECIAL ABOUT
RAIN FOREST PLANTS?

Tropical rain forests around the world have different plant species, but they also have a lot in common. Here are a few of their shared features:

Many Layers of Life   Rain forest trees grow to different heights within the forest, giving the forest a layered look, called stratification. A tropical rain forest typically has four layers, more than most temperate deciduous forests. These layers are: emergents, canopy, understory, and forest floor. Each of these layers has distinctive animals and plants.

Woodiness   Rain forest plants are constantly competing for light. That's one reason you'll find gigantic trees, dinner-plate-sized leaves, and 2,600-foot- (800-meter-) long vines in these forests. To support the weight of these light-seeking and light-catching structures, many plants develop sturdy, woody stems and trunks.

Species Diversity   Rain forests contain more different kinds of animals and plant species than any other biome on earth. In just one 25-acre (10-hectare) patch of Malaysian forest, scientists found 750 different tree species. That's more native tree species than in the whole of the United States and Canada! A patch of rain forest typically has 10 times more tree species and 5 times more bird species than a temperate forest patch of the same size.

PLANT STRATEGIES

In the rainy season, rain forest plants often receive more water than they need. That can cause trouble. Water collecting on leaves can weigh a plant down; constant wetness can promote the growth of mold, causing decay. So, to get rid of water, many rain forest plants have slick coatings, shapes that easily shed rain, and spoutlike "drip tips" that help drain water from leaf surfaces.

Radical Roots   In tropical rain forests, nutrients aren't stored in the soil. They're held in the plants and animals of the forest. To gather nutrients, rain forest trees send out tiny roots that spread across the ground in a spongy layer. This root layer catches decaying leaves, fruits, and other falling organic materials, then absorbs nutrients from them.

Fungi Partners   Many rain forest trees, and trees in other biomes, have mycorrhizae, a mutualistic relationship with fungi. A mutualistic relationship is one in which both par-

Drip tips are just one way rain forest plants adapt to their environment.

ties benefit from the arrangement. In this case, the fungi form threadlike extensions that grow through the tree's roots and help the roots absorb water and nutrients better. In return, the fungi live on sugars the tree provides.

A Little Support   Roots do more than just gather water and nutrients. They help support a tree's weight. Tropical rain forest trees form buttresses—roots that grow out from the trunk, aboveground. Spreading out like the folds of a swirled skirt, these buttresses create a wide, stable base for the tree. These structures may also help gather nutrients.

THE BATTLE OF THE PLANTS

In the struggle to survive, rain forest plants have evolved some pretty amazing defenses. Consider these rain forest plants' adaptations:

Chemical Warfare To protect themselves from plant eaters, some trees produce tannins and other difficult-to-digest chemical compounds in their leaves and seeds. And lots of rain forest plants release chemicals into the soil to poison other plants. This keeps the other plants out of their space.

A Standing Army Strong biting jaws and sprays of formic acid greet intruders who touch the *Cecropia* tree. These trees are protected from leaf-eating insects by armies of ants. In return for this service, ants get sweet liquid droplets secreted by the tree, and homes in cavities within the tree.

Fake Eggs, Falling Tendrils, and Other Tricks Passion flower vines have several surprising ways of discouraging leaf-eating caterpillars. These vines mimic the leaf patterns of nearby trees in order to hide. They also grow tendrils upon which butterflies lay eggs, then drop the tendrils to get rid of the eggs! Some passion flower vines form fake yellow caterpillar eggs on their stems; egg-laying butterflies see the fake eggs and pass by, looking for an unoccupied place to lay their eggs.

PLANTS LIVING UPON PLANTS

Up near the tops of many rain forest trees, you'll find ponds complete with wriggling insect larvae, tadpoles, lizards, and even resident crabs. These mini-wetlands are inside bromeliads—plants whose leaves funnel water into a cup-shaped depression in their middle.

Bromeliads are just one of the many kinds of epiphytes. Epiphytes are plants that grow on other plants and send no roots to the ground. Ferns, lichens, orchids, and bromeliads can all grow as epiphytes, living on rain forest tree branches.

To get the minerals they need for photosynthesis, some epiphytes dangle roots to gather minerals from dust in the air and rain. An epiphyte called the bird's nest fern forms a bowl shape that catches leaves, bird droppings, and other organic matter. Within the bowl, the leaves form a miniature compost pile. And the plant's roots grow inward to get the nutrients it needs.

Space Invaders Epiphytes don't directly compete for nutrients with the tree they live upon. But they do weigh the tree down, sometimes causing branches to break. Insects that live within epiphytes can damage the tree, too. So, to get rid of these space invaders, some trees shed their bark, or secrete toxins that discourage epiphyte growth. Others cultivate a relationship with ants that chew off any epiphytes that try to grow on the tree's limbs.

SWINGIN' LIANAS AND VINES
Looping, twisting, and climbing, lianas and vines tangle among rain forest treetops. Lianas look and grow much like vines, but they have sturdier, woody tissues like trees. Using curling tendrils, barbed thorns, or clasping roots, these plants climb over trees, getting a "boost" to the forest canopy, where there's more sunlight.

STRANGLING FIGS
In Panama, people call it *matapalo*—the "tree killer"; others just call it the strangler fig. Both names are well earned. The strangler fig is a plant that sprouts from sticky seeds deposited in animal droppings on tree branches. Unlike epiphytes, strangler figs send finger-thick roots down to the

These climbers are inside a hollow strangler fig, where a tree once stood.

ground and into the soil. Then its shoots grow and tangle around the trunk of the host tree. Eventually, the fig's leaves block the tree's sunlight, and its vines choke off the tree's circulation. The tree dies and rots, leaving a hollow, tree-shaped form made by the fig's tangled, merged vines. Despite their reputation as stranglers, these fig trees play an important role in the rain forest community by providing fruits for wildlife throughout the year.

POLLINATION PROMOTION

In the rain forest, individuals of a plant species often grow far apart—even acres apart. Some canopy trees and emergent trees use wind to carry their pollen from one to another. But this method can be somewhat hit or miss. So, most other plants use animals or insects to carry pollen around instead.

Specific Spots   Flowers and their pollinators can match almost as closely as a lock and key. A *Heliconia* flower's shape fits a hummingbird's bill. And when a hummingbird puts its head into a *Heliconia* flower to sip nectar, the flower dabs pollen on the hummingbird's body. It brushes off a little pollen, too. Each *Heliconia* species dabs its pollen on a certain part of the bird's body, so the pollen of different species doesn't mix.

Many flowers cater just to specific "customers." Smelly, dull-colored, free-hanging, night-blooming flowers attract bats. Long, trumpet-shaped flowers are more likely to be visited by hummingbirds, who have long bills. By

The long, curved bill of this hummingbird allows it to drink from Heliconia *flowers.*

Parrots spread the seeds of the fruit they eat.

using animal "couriers" in this way, plants ensure their pollen isn't wasted on other species of plants. Some flowers actually trick insects into visiting them by mimicking the smell or appearance of insects of the opposite sex!

SEED SPREADERS

Fruit is made to be eaten. It's a plant's way of getting an animal to carry its seeds around. Animals act as seed dispersers—spreading seeds to new areas, where they can grow up but won't compete with the parent plant. When a parrot or monkey dines on a fleshy fruit, the fruit's tiny, sturdy seeds pass right through the animal's digestive system. When the bird flies to another tree, or the monkey wanders off, the seeds are deposited in its droppings. (The droppings also serve as handy fertilizer for the seedling.)

Seed Snatchers   Some plants don't have edible fruits—only seeds. These seeds may be dropped to the ground, spread by wind or water, carried by animals, or catapulted by exploding seed pods. Unfortunately for the plant, animals often like to eat these seeds, especially oily ones such as cashews and Brazil nuts. Unlike seeds in edible fruits, these seeds are destroyed if an animal eats them. So, to defend against the seed eaters, plants have evolved seeds with tough outer shells. But many animals, in turn, have evolved strong seed-cracking jaws or beaks. In an odd turn of events, one tree—the Brazil nut tree—is actually helped by a seed destroying rodent called the agouti. This tree produces so many seeds that the rabbit-sized agouti eats its fill, then buries some for later. Fortunately for the tree, the agouti doesn't have a perfect memory, so it leaves some seeds in the ground, and these seeds later sprout and grow.

THE GENERATION GAP

Rain forest trees don't live forever. High winds, lightning, termites, old age, or just the weight of rain-soaked mosses and epiphytes may cause a tree to topple. Its fall may also bring down other trees connected to it by lianas.

After a tree falls, sunlight streams into the newly created forest gap, increasing temperatures and drying the air. Seeds that lay dormant in the soil sprout and grow. Seeds from nearby trees and seeds dropped by animals colonize the sunny gap, too. In time, this gap begins to look like the rest of the forest, once again. But this may take a century or more. Small gaps produced by tree falls or native farming may regrow quickly. But very large gaps produced by logging or other activities may never reseed and recover.

5
RAIN FOREST
ANIMALS

Don't be disappointed if you're walking in the rain forest and all you spot at first is a bunch of leaves and tree trunks. You may be seeing more than you realize. That's because in the rain forest what looks like a dead leaf may be a butterfly. What looks like a broken branch may be a bird. And what looks like only a hanging clump of moss may actually be an algae-covered sloth!

Natural disguise—called camouflage—is just one of the many adaptations of rain forest animals. In these forests you'll find brightly colored frogs with poisons in their skin, furry monkeys who use their tails like extra arms, and butterflies whose wings spread almost a foot wide (30 centimeters). But that's only a small sampling of the rain forest's treasures. This biome is full of unusual and exciting animals whose looks and behavior are almost too strange to imagine.

CRAZY COLORS AND DISGUISES

Over millions of years, rain forest prey animals have evolved ways to evade predators. To hide from insect eaters, leafhoppers resemble thorns. Katydids, walking sticks, and moths look like twigs, leaves, or bark. If fitting in doesn't work, some creatures use another strategy: the startle defense. Butterflies who look like dead leaves when their wings are closed often have bright colors on their inner wing surfaces. If a predator should get too close, the butter-

This poison arrow frog's bright color is a warning to predators—stay away!

fly opens its wings to flash its bright colors. This may startle the predator, perhaps giving the butterfly time to escape.

Natural Advertising Bright colors have other uses, too. Poison arrow frogs come in a rainbow of bright colors—yellow, red, and blue—that tell potential predators they're poisonous. This kind of negative advertising is used by insects, too. A bird may eat the first heliconid butterfly it sees. But these butterflies are so bad tasting that the bird probably won't eat another. Bright color patterns on this species will remind the predator of the bad experience it had the last time it ate a heliconid. There's even another kind of butterfly—a nonpoisonous one—that mimics the heliconid's patterns. In this way, it takes advantage of the heliconid's bad reputation, and avoids being eaten.

Surprise! Prey animals aren't the only ones who try to fit in with the background. Camouflage can give predators a real advantage in the hunt. The dappled coat of a clouded

In the wet rain forest world, frogs don't have to lay their eggs in a puddle or pond. Some use their hind legs to whip up a foam where their eggs can stay moist. Others lay their eggs on leaves where they don't dry out because the tropical rain forest is so humid.

Poison arrow frogs lay their eggs on wet leaves, then guard them until they hatch. After the eggs hatch, the male frog carries the tadpoles on his back to tiny pools within bromeliads up in trees. Hopping along in the tree-tops, he carefully deposits one tadpole in each bromelaid pool. Later on, the female comes by and drops off unfertilized eggs, which serve as food for the tadpoles.

leopard helps it hide in the shadows. Mottled brown coils keep the fer-de-lance snake hidden until its prey is in striking range. And a matamata's folded features make it look like rotten leaves floating in a stream, instead of what it really is: a turtle hunting for frogs.

SPECIAL RELATIONSHIPS

In the Central American rain forest, ants stand guard over hundreds of treehoppers—insects who drink juices from plant stems. Why do these ants protect the treehoppers? Because the treehoppers leave sugary droppings the ants eat. The relationship between the ants and the treehoppers is an example of mutualism; both benefit from the arrangement.

Crowd Followers   When army ants are on the march, birds, lizards, mice, and insects scramble to get out of the way. But antbirds and other insect-eating birds follow the mob. They're not after the ants, though. They just take advantage of the confusion an army ant raid causes. They

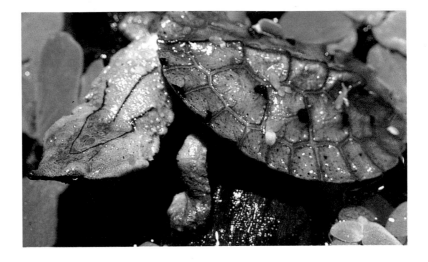

Hidden by its leafy-looking hide, the river-dwelling matamata can snap up unwary fish.

snap up insects that would normally be motionless, camouflaged, and much harder to find.

Hitchhikers   Hundreds of species of hummingbird flower mites live in trumpet-shaped flowers and eat nectar. What's really odd about these mites is their mode of travel. When a hummingbird visits their flower for a sip, they hop on the hummingbird's beak or feathers. The hummingbird flies to the next flower, and the mite hops off in its new home.

FOREST TALK

In a forest, sound bounces off trees, scatters among leaves, and is absorbed even by the ground itself. And with all the noise of other animals—insects humming, primates calling, birds singing, and frogs chirping—it can be hard to single out an individual animal above the crowd.

To get around this trouble, birds and monkeys have evolved calls that carry well in the part of the forest where

When they're not resting, these tree-trunk travelers, called sifakas, are capable of spectacular leaps from tree to tree.

they live. Birds low in the forest emit pure-toned whistles, while birds higher up in the forest, where sound carries farther, use more varied melodies. Monkeys may climb to branches to make their calls in the clearest space possible. And howler monkeys, who can be heard over half a mile (about a kilometer) away, call most often in the cool morning; calls travel farther in cooler air.

Animals find other ways to communicate as well. A female butterfly's potent perfume can travel for over a mile (almost 2 kilometers), attracting a mate. Lemurs mark their territories using scent glands on their wrists and below their tails to deposit their own personal perfume. And lots of tropical birds get their message across with brightly colored feathers and showy movements.

TRAVEL IN THE TREETOPS

Tropical treetops are rich with mammal species—from giant squirrels to flying lemurs, to pangolins, sun bears, and anteaters. This abundance makes sense, because the upper reaches of the tropical forest are where most of the food is located. There are even "highways": clear areas on branches where so many animals walk that epiphytes cannot grow.

Arm Swinging   To move about in the treetops, rain forest mammals have evolved a variety of methods of locomotion. Primates such as gibbons and spider monkeys brachiate— swing arm to arm from tree branch to tree branch, like a kid on playground monkey bars. Other primates don't swing; they cling, and then leap. Tarsiers, lemurs like indris and sifakas, and other clingers and leapers zigzag through the forest, clinging to one tree trunk, then leaping to another, and so on, and so on.

Hanging Around   To help them balance in the trees, certain tropical porcupines and monkeys have a prehensile tail. A prehensile tail is a tail capable of grasping things. Wrapped around a branch, it provides extra stability. Spider

*Adapted for life aboveground, a spider monkey
swings through the trees with her young.*

monkeys often hang just by their tails, leaving their hands free to pull apart fruit as they dine upside down.

FOREST FEASTING

"You are what you eat!" many people insist. Well, that may not be quite true. But the shape, size, form and behavior of many rain forest animals does have a lot to do with their eating habits.

Leaf Lovers   Leaves are a nutritious, easy-to-find food. But there's a catch: leaves are made of cellulose, which is hard to digest. Sloths, colobus monkeys, and other large leaf eaters have special bacteria in their stomachs that break down cellulose. This method takes a lot of time, though; so leaf eaters tend to be slower moving and less energetic than animals that eat fruit or insects. Sloths may spend as much as 18 hours a day just hanging motionless in the trees!

A leafy diet doesn't work well for most birds, however. Birds need high-energy, easy-to-digest foods to power their flight. But one rain forest bird—the hoatzin—eats leaves anyway. It's a terrible flier, yet it seems to get along just fine. People call it the "stinkbird" because the fermenting leaves inside it make it smell like cow manure!

Fruit Eaters and Nectar Sippers   Fruit is available year-round in tropical forests, not just in the summer and fall, as in temperate regions. So frugivores—fruit-eating special-ists—are common in rain forests. Many animals also dine on another sweet food—nectar. Nectar is mostly sugar and water, a high-energy drink that keeps hummingbirds, bees, bats, and wasps coming back for more. To balance their diets, hummingbirds snap up protein-rich insects as well.

Sap Drinkers and Gum Chewers   Clinging to tree trunks, primates such as pygmy marmosets, bush babies, and some lemurs gnaw away bark in order to drink tree sap. They may also chew and swallow gum—a sticky liquid some trees produce to discourage insects. (That's where our chewing gum first came from—a tree gum called chicle.)

Power Play   Rain forest predators naturally have the tools needed to catch their prey. A jaguar's strong jaws allow it to kill prey with a crushing bite to the skull. A boa constrictor's muscular coils help it hug its prey, squeezing it to death. While a giant anteater's barbed, sticky, 24-inch- (60-centimeter-) long tongue is perfect for lapping up termites from nests.

Poisons and Traps   Scorpions, spiders, and some snakes use poisons to slow down their prey, stop it from struggling, and make it easier to digest. Orb weaving spiders spin enormous webs, with silk so strong people in New Guinea use it as fishing line. Some tropical spiders even catch and eat birds!

Fungi Farmers   Ants called leaf-cutter ants are fungi farmers. They cut pieces of leaves and store them in their nest. Then they add fungi to their leaf pile. These fungi break down the leaves, grow, and multiply. Eventually the ants have a sizeable fungi feast.

BE AN ENTOMOLOGIST

An entomologist is a scientist who studies insects. As insects are among the most numerous members of the animal kingdom, you can find insects to study just about anywhere you are, night or day. To gather insects in the rain forest, entomologists often go out at night and set up a light behind a white sheet. Just like moths attracted to a porch light, many insects will fly to the lighted sheet. You can use the same technique to gather insects in your area.

Materials:
- White sheet
- Strings to hang the sheet or people to hold it
- Light source—either a strong flashlight, an outdoor porch light, or a car with headlights on
- Jar for collecting insects
- Field guide for identifying insects

Hang the sheet a foot to several feet (30 centimeters to a full meter) from your light source, so that much of the sheet is illuminated by the light. You can also have people take turns holding the sheet, if you wish. Insects will fly toward the light and land on the sheet. Gently knock or brush the insects off the sheet and into a jar.

Use a container with small air holes in it to keep the insects for a short time until you are finished studying them and can release them. A glass jar covered with cheesecloth secured by a rubber band works well. Remember: like other animals, some insects are rare and endangered. So learn about the insects in your area and handle them with care. Be sure not to disturb luna moths or praying mantises.

RAIN FOREST ANIMAL ADAPTATIONS

Many of the adaptations discussed in this chapter aren't found exclusively in rain forests. But often they reach their height of complexity in this biome. Perhaps one reason is the complexity of the forest itself—its many layers, and its many species. Or perhaps this richness of adaptation is because rain forest species have had longer to develop than those in many other biomes.

RAIN FOREST
COMMUNITIES

Without a hummingbird to pollinate it, the *Heliconia* would not set seed and reproduce. Without the nectar from the *Heliconia* flower, the hummingbird would have to search longer and harder to find a meal.

The rain forest, and all biomes for that matter, are made up of seemingly endless numbers of such interconnections. Each animal, plant, fungus, and bacterium plays a role within a biological community. The tropical rain forest community is a complex layer cake of life, which has so many species, and so many biological "goings on," it boggles the mind. For this very reason, botanists, ecologists, zoologists, and other scientists find the tropical rain forest to be one of the most exciting biomes to study.

LAYERS OF LIFE

To at least some scientists, the rain forest community appears to have divisions—layers of life. Here's a quick rundown of the typical rain forest layers and their characteristics:

The Emergents   These tallest of rain forest trees may reach heights of 75 to 250 feet (22 to 76 meters). Their crowns, shaped like open umbrellas, stick out here and there above the main "roof" of the forest—the canopy layer. Emergent trees get the full force of drying winds, hot sun, and soaking rains. As a result, emergent trees tend to have small, leathery leaves that retain water. Up in an emergent tree, where the view is good, a harpy eagle might build its nest and keep a lookout for prey below.

The Canopy   The smaller crowns of these 40- to 70-foot- (more than 10- to 20-meter-) tall trees form the roof of the forest, blocking most of the sun from the plants below. Like the emergent layer, much of the canopy gets the full force of sun, wind, and hard rain. Sun-loving bromeliads, flattened-leaf cacti, ferns, and other plants grow on canopy branches. Here, where there's plenty of sun, 90 percent of the rain forest's photosynthesis occurs. Many tree leaves contain potent poisons to protect them from plant eaters. This is the most active forest layer, where sloths, howler monkeys, opossums, anteaters, rats, marmosets, and a wide range of birds and other animals make their homes.

The Understory   In the dim light under the canopy, thinner-trunked trees, with narrow crowns shaped like closed umbrellas, form another layer. These trees' leaves are larger, to catch sunlight in the dim, moist interior. Leaf-eating animals dine here because the leaves are large and often less poisonous than those in the canopy. Insect-eating birds travel tree trunks and branches, ferreting out insects that feed on moist or rotting wood.

The Forest Floor   Only 1 percent or less of the light received by the canopy reaches this layer. So it's no wonder very little plant life is found here. Ferns and small, broad-leafed plants grow here. Among the maze of tiny tree roots, a host of fungi, termites, bacteria, and other creatures make meals of rotten leaves, fruit, animal droppings, branches, and other organic matter that falls from above. In places where tree falls create gaps and sunlight streams in, dense shrubs and grasses fill in and provide food for herbivores.

WHAT A WEB

If you think unraveling a spiderweb would be tough, try tracing out the connections among tropical rain forest animals. Just one tree may have 43 species of ants and 30 or more species of bromeliads living upon it. Each bromeliad may have a pool with insects inside—both insect predators and insect prey. Even in a rotted center of a tree trunk, bats can roost, owls hide, and thousands of insects crawl, burrow, and climb.

The producers of the forests are trees, bromeliads, vines, and undergrowth. They make the leaves, fruits, and other plant products that plant-eating consumers, from insects to elephants, eat. Secondary consumers, the forest's meat eaters, come in many forms, too—from damselflies to snakes, anteaters to warblers. Jaguars, tigers, harpy eagles, and even humans can serve as top consumers. After scavengers such as vultures have had their meals, the great workers of the forest, the decomposers, do their work.

ENERGY FLOW

With all this activity, it's a good thing there are decomposers such as fungi, bacteria, and earthworms around. Otherwise the forest floor might be clogged with branches, leaves, droppings, and other organic material that hadn't rotted. And without these creatures to decompose dead material, the forest wouldn't have enough minerals and organic matter to help trees and other plants grow.

Fortunately, there are plenty of decomposers to do the job. Termites eat wood, with the help of their intestinal bacteria and protozoans that break down this tough-to-digest substance. Countless numbers of fungi, protozoans, bacteria, and earthworms help decompose materials, too. In moist, warm rain forests, these decomposers accomplish their task at top speed. Rain forest leaf litter can be decomposed in only about six weeks—one-sixtieth of the time it takes in a northern coniferous forest.

Here, on the rain forest's nutrient-poor soils, minerals needed for life, such as calcium, carbon, potassium, and nitrogen, are snatched up quickly by organisms in every part of the food chain. That's the only way such a rich, diverse group of animals and plants can live on such poor soil.

MEASURES OF LIFE

It's obvious when you look at a rain forest that there's more "stuff" growing in it than grows in a desert. To measure such a difference, biologists measure plant biomass—the weight of the roots, shoots, leaves, tree trunks, and other plant material that exists in a certain area. Rain forests are very productive; each year a tropical rain forest produces 300 to 1,100 ounces of plant matter per square foot (1,000 to 3,500 grams per square meter) per year. The desert only produces 3 to 8 ounces of plant matter per square foot (10 to 25 grams per square meter) per year.

The big surprise is that most of this extra productivity isn't made up of heavy tree trunks and limbs. It's made up of leaves—layers and layers of leaves that gather light within the forest. Plants in warm, tropical areas generally use more energy just to maintain their tissues. So lots of leaves are needed as factories to produce the sugars plants need for running their daily activities.

DIVERSITY

More than half the world's plant and animal species live in rain forests. There are so many plant and animal species that scientists discover new ones almost every day. Just 2.47 acres (a hectare) of forest may contain 42,000 different species of insects. And 43 species of ants have been found on just one tree!

In fact, rain forests are the most species-diverse biomes in the world. Their position on the earth—straddling the equator—may have something to do with this species diversity. If you traveled from either of the earth's Poles

· WHERE THE ACTION IS ·

For many years, the rain forest canopy frustrated scientists. While they walked along on the rain forest floor, much of the life of the rain forest was going on literally above their heads—out of reach. To really know the rain forest scientists felt they must find a way to explore this layer. Here are some techniques scientists have used to study the forest canopy:

• Some entomologists study the life of the canopy layer by fogging the canopy with a biodegradable insecticide. Thousands of insects fall to the ground and can then be identified and studied. As many as 1,700 species of insects may be found on one tree.

• These days, many scientists use ropes, climbing gear, and ladders to climb up to platforms and walkways built among trees. One of the difficulties with these aerial constructions is that termites quickly eat any wooden parts of the structures. Modern walkways often use lightweight rope suspension systems.

• To study animals up high, scientists on Panama's Barro Colorado Island have installed a building crane that lifts them to where they want to go.

• In French Guiana, scientists used a blimp to gently lower a 6,460-square-foot (600-square-meter) air-filled raft onto the rain forest canopy. Nestled atop the canopy, its weight held equally by the tops of many trees, the raft served as a good base for scientists' studies.

• Treetop work can be dangerous, but that isn't stopping scientists from heading for the canopy to do their studies. As far as they're concerned, the treetops are where the action is.

toward the equator, you'd see that the number of animal and plant species generally increases along your journey.

What are the reasons for this increasing plant and animal diversity toward the equator? Part of the reason may be that the sun shines directly toward the equator, so there's more solar energy available for photosynthesis. More photosynthesis means more plant food, which can feed more animals. Having fairly constant temperature and rainfall conditions helps, too. Plants and animals don't need to adapt to strong seasonal influences, so they can evolve lifestyles that would never be possible in an environment that shifted from cold to hot to cold.

TAKE A HIKE IN THE TROPICAL RAIN FOREST

In a tropical rain forest, the weather is generally quite warm. (Unless you're high up on a mountain, in a cloud forest.) So wear lightweight pants and a lightweight shirt, plus good, strong, waterproof boots. Tucking your pants in these boots will help keep leeches out. In the rainy season, you'll need rain gear, including a hat. And as always, be sure to know where you're going, tell someone of your plans, bring a map, and carry enough food and water to keep your energy level high. Here are just a few of the things you can look for, smell for, and listen for on a tropical rain forest hike:

- Footprints of a jaguarundi near a stream's edge;
- The twangs of frogs calling for mates;
- Hummingbirds zipping through the forest, on their way to bright red flowers;
- A green, algae-covered sloth in the canopy overhead;
- The sound of whirring wings as insects try to escape army ants on a raid;
- Leaf mimic butterflies gathered at a puddle;
- The hanging nests of an oropendula bird;
- Deep marks on trees, where a jaguar has sharpened its claws;
- A column of leaf-cutter ants carrying cut leaves in their jaws;
- The deafening roar of a howler monkey;
- A tiny, insect-filled pool inside a bromeliad plant.

Yet another reason for the rain forest's diversity is its wetness. The availability of water—one of the main ingredients of any plant's or animal's life—makes possible many unusual lifestyles that wouldn't work in drier climates. The layers of the forest also give animals many separate, unique areas where different species can live. Scientists believe the variety of species in the rain forest probably also has to do with the forest's history, the way this biome has grown and shrunk as the climate changed over thousands of years. For now, scientists still have many questions about which factors have been the most important in creating such a diversity of species within the rain forest.

A FOREST IN FRAGMENTS

Even if a forest is not cut down, it can be destroyed by logging roads and other developments that slice the land up into small patches. This fragmentation can make a forest a less useful habitat for species. When their territories are disrupted, or their population numbers become too small, many species cannot survive.

7
PEOPLE AND THE
RAIN FOREST

While researching in Madagascar's rain forest, a scientist got a bad cough that wouldn't go away. Back in the United States, none of her doctors could help her. But when she returned to Madagascar, a local person made a tea of rain forest leaves that cured her for good.

This medical knowledge may seem amazing to us, but it's all a part of rain forest survival. If you talk to Kuikuru people from central Brazil, it's likely they'll be able to name a couple of hundred tree species. Even more important, they can tell you which ones are better for building houses and which ones are better for building fires. They are also aware of the food web around them—which fruits monkeys prefer and which species eat certain leaves. This knowledge is vital whether they're gathering fruits and herbs, or hunting animals for meat.

RAIN FOREST PEOPLE

The Kuikuru are not the only culture who live close to the land and know a lot about the forest. An estimated 1,000 indigenous—native—tribes live in rain forests around the world. At one time, there were about six million indigenous people living just in the Amazon forest alone. Today only 250,000 survive in this area, because over the last five centuries, explorers, conquerors, and other settlers who moved into the forest have wiped out millions of these native people. Many indigenous people were killed outright; others died from diseases they caught from the new settlers.

Gold Rush in the Amazon Threats to indigenous peoples' way of life continue today. In Brazil, for instance, thousands of gold miners are illegally moving into the Yanomami tribe's land. Mercury used in mining is poisoning streams where the Yanomami fish. And the gold miners are exposing the Yanomami to deadly diseases. So far, the Brazilian government has been unsuccessful in their attempts to stop miners from moving onto Yanomami lands. In August 1993, gold miners slaughtered more than 70 Yanomami people in order to gain control of their lands.

In the race to save their culture and their lives, indigenous people are learning to use modern tools. Some are using video cameras to document the destruction on their lands. And coalitions of native people are traveling from forests to the cities to protest the invasions of their lands, as well as unfavorable laws and court rulings.

The clothing worn by this Yanomami family shows a mixture of ancient and modern influences.

The Changing Amazon   Rain forest inhabitants today have a mixture of origins and a wide variety of lifestyles. Some indigenous tribes continue to follow their traditional hunting, gathering, or farming way of life. But as their traditional lands are destroyed or fragmented, many are forced to live in villages and adopt a modern lifestyle.

In government sponsored programs, or on their own initiative, settlers from outside the forest are moving into rain forest areas. Lured by the dream of a better life, farmers, cattle ranchers, gold miners, and loggers are moving farther and farther into the forest. Most of these settlers practice a type of slash-and-burn agriculture that is very damaging to the land.

SLASH-AND-BURN

Slash-and-burn agriculture is an ancient type of farming used by millions of people all over the tropics. In slash-and-burn, farmers cut down the forest trees, then burn the undergrowth, called "slash." When the burned ground has cooled, crops are planted, and ash from the burning gives crops a burst of nutrients that helps them grow quickly. But this quick growth lasts for only a little while. Farming in these patches works for 2 to 7 years, depending on what crops are planted and how they are tended. But once the patch becomes unproductive, the farmer must shift to a new area and cut down another patch of rain forest.

The Good Side   Slash-and-burn agriculture isn't all bad. If practiced properly, it mimics the forest's natural ecology. Like a tree that falls in the forest, slash-and-burn agriculture opens up a sunny forest gap that can later fill in with plants. People such as the Lacandon Maya of Mexico practice a type of slash-and-burn agriculture called agroforestry. They plant vegetables, fruit trees, and native plants to attract wildlife for hunting. Once they abandon a plot of land, it's allowed to lie fallow, to reseed and regrow, like a natural

· WILD CURES ·

One day your life may be saved by a rain forest plant. Two-thirds of the medicines people use today were first made from rain forest plants. Three-quarters of those were discovered through ethnobotany—studying the traditional uses of plants by native peoples around the world.

Thanks to a small pink-flowered plant called periwinkle that grows in Madagascar, many leukemia patients recover and live long, healthy lives. Vincristine and vinblastine, found in the Madagascan rosy periwinkle, are used in chemotherapy to help cure the disease. Numerous other rain forest plants are being investigated for their healing properties.

Why do plants make chemicals like these? To defend themselves from hungry plant eaters. These chemicals can make leaves bad tasting, belly sickening, or otherwise poisonous to animals. But one insect's poison may be a human being's food additive or medicine. Morphine, tannin, and caffeine are just a few of the thousands of compounds produced by rain forest plants. Because there are so many insects and plant eaters in rain forests, rain forest species are more likely to produce these chemicals than plant species that live in other biomes.

forest gap. The Lacandon Maya's techniques may be the key to better farming in the future.

The Bad Side   For now, much of the slash-and-burn farming in the tropics is not very productive and is damaging to the environment. A growing population, lack of land, and pressure to produce crops lead farmers to recut patches too soon. Patches are usually too large and close together, so there's not as much natural forest to help reseed, protect, and regrow the cleared patch. Also, today's farmers may grow just one or two plant types, not the diversity of small crops, trees, and native plants the Maya use. And new rain forest settlers often start farms on areas with the poorest soils. Knowledgeable tropical farmers carefully choose their crop location.

THIS FRAGILE FOREST

Every second, more than an acre (two-fifths of a hectare) of rain forest is destroyed. An estimated 50 million acres (more than 20 million hectares) are wiped out each year. Recent photos of the earth from space show that the destruction is happening much faster than scientists thought only a few years ago. It's a global problem that cannot be ignored.

WHY SHOULD *YOU* CARE ABOUT RAIN FOREST DESTRUCTION?

You may be wondering why you should care about rain forest destruction, especially if you don't live near a rain forest. Some reasons people are concerned about the loss of these forests are:

Biodiversity   Rain forests are estimated to hold half of the earth's species. Losing these species is like losing all the rare books in a library, and all the knowledge they contain. This diversity of species may be important for our future. In our changing world, we may need the rain forest's genetic wealth of information to adapt to changing global conditions.

Rainfall   Rain forests produce and recycle much of their own rain. Scientists believe that if the rain forest is cut down, rainfall in the tropics will decrease. In these dry conditions, not only will the rain forest not grow back, but other tropical growing areas may suffer as well.

The Giant Heat Pump   The rain forest plays an important part in the global heat pump that passes tropical heat to temperate regions such as North America. Rain forest destruction could disrupt this heat pump, changing global weather patterns.

Global Warming   Burning the rain forest contributes to global warming. In some years as much as one-quarter of the world's human-created greenhouse gases have come from the burning of tropical rain forests.

Indigenous People   The rain forest not only holds a diversity of species, it's home to many different and unique cultures. If the rain forest is destroyed, these people's cultures—their language, their knowledge, their skills, their way of life, will disappear.

THE IMMEDIATE CAUSES OF
RAIN FOREST DESTRUCTION

The causes of rain forest destruction are many, and they vary from place to place.

Harvest for Timber and Fuel   The collection of wood for fuel, furniture, and other products is threatening the world's rain forests. Southeast Asia has been almost entirely deforested for logs to make everything from furniture to disposable chopsticks. Because these forests are almost gone, the timber industry is expected to increase their harvest in Africa and South America in the next few years, threatening rain forests there.

Clearing for Agriculture   Slash-and-burn agriculture is destroying rain forests worldwide, but especially in economically poor, overpopulated countries such as Madagascar.

Clearing for Cattle Ranching   Much of Central America's rain forest has already been turned into grazing land for cattle. Yet these lands are nutrient poor and can only support cattle for a short time.

Flooding During Dam Construction Planned hydroelectric projects in Brazil will permanently flood millions of acres of tropical forest.

There are other causes of rain forest destruction. Rain forests are also cut down to make room for houses, cities, mining operations, and other activities. Air pollution, water pollution, and other by-products of human development also degrade the rain forest habitat. And illegal collection of animals for pets and wildlife products is wiping out many already threatened rain forest species.

DEEP-ROOTED CAUSES

Mining, cattle ranching, and slash-and-burn agriculture are some of the immediate causes of rain forest destruction. But there's much more to the story. After all, why is cattle ranching so widespread in tropical forests? And why are so many people moving into rain forests to farm land? The answers to these questions lie in the many underlying causes of rain forest destruction. Human population growth is a major cause, but poverty and unequal land distribution also aggravate the problem.

Government policies have also been a big factor. In the Philippines, Brazil, Costa Rica, and elsewhere, people get ownership of rain forest land only if they "improve" it. In most places, "improvement" means clearing off the forest. International financial forces have also made things worse. Over the last few decades, many tropical countries borrowed billions of dollars from international banks for dams, power plants, and other projects. Now these nations are having a hard time paying back their loans. Often these countries allow environmentally unwise development so they can get enough tax money to pay off their debts.

SEEDS OF HOPE

The problem of rain forest destruction is so serious that at times it can seem depressing to think about. But there *is* hope for the future. Just look at some of the things people are doing around the world to save rain forests:

Park It!   In Madagascar, the new Ranomafana National Park will preserve rare lemurs and other species in a hilly slice of eastern rain forest. The park project includes plans to help local people around the park improve forestry and rice growing. Small loans help native Malagasy set up businesses that benefit from park tourists. And a "buffer zone" around the park is a partial preserve, where native people can carry out traditional activities.

Go Nuts!   Brazil nuts and natural rubber are just a few of the products that can be sustainably harvested from the forest. That means they can be gathered year after year without significant damage to the forest. The Brazilian government plans to set aside four large "extractive reserves" where these products could be gathered, giving people a way to make money from the forest without destroying it.

Swapping Debt for Nature   Conservationists in money-rich nations are helping rain-forest-rich countries save their forests. For example, several years ago American and Canadian environmental groups helped pay off part of Costa Rica's debt. In return, Costa Rica agreed to set aside some of its rain forest in parks and reserves.

N.G.O.   These letters stand for nongovernmental organization. These grassroots environmental groups are popping up all over the world. In Brazil, one organization, Funatura, has helped establish and manage wildlife sanctuaries.

Healing the Forest   On Barro Colorado Island, Panama, scientists are working on a project to learn how to grow 700 species of rain forest plants. Hopefully, this project will help in future reforestation of damaged rain forest land.

Tropical Training   In Ecuador, Madagascar, Panama, Costa Rica, and other countries, international scientists are helping train people who live near rain forests to gather scientific data. Once trained, these skilled local naturalists can help carry out scientific studies. In addition, some conservation projects fund exchange programs so that promising university students in rain forest countries can gain additional scientific training overseas.

The conservation efforts listed above are only a few of the thousands of rain-forest-saving projects going on worldwide. From Brazil to Borneo to Buffalo, New York, people are chipping in to help preserve rain forests. But for these forests to remain healthy, green, and growing in the future, conservation efforts will have to be expanded, and quickly. You can get involved in saving one of the most exciting and colorful biomes on earth!

RESOURCES AND WHAT
YOU CAN DO TO HELP

Here's what you can do to help preserve rain forests:

• Learn more by reading books and watching videos and television programs about the rain forest. Check your local library, bookstore, and video store for resources. Here are just a few of the books and magazine articles available for further reading:

Diversity and the Tropical Rain Forest by John Terborgh (Scientific American Library, 1992).

In the Rainforest by Catherine Caufield (Knopf, 1984).

Life above the Forest Floor by Donald Perry (Simon and Schuster, 1986).

People of the Tropical Rain Forest: In Association with Smithsonian Institution Traveling Exhibit Service, edited by Julie Sloan Denslow and Christine Padoch (University of California Press, 1988).

"Rain Forest Canopy: The High Frontier," by E. O. Wilson (*National Geographic*, December 1991).

Tropical Nature: Life and Death in the Rain Forests of Central and South America by Adrian Forsyth and Ken Miyata (Macmillan, 1987).

• For more information on rain forests, and what you can do to help preserve them, write the following organizations:

Conservation International
1015 18th Street NW
Suite 1000
Washington, DC 20036
Phone 1-202-429-5660

Rainforest Action Network
450 Sansome Street
Suite 700
San Francisco, CA 94111
Phone 1-415-398-4404

If you like the job these groups are doing, consider becoming a member.

• To order rain forest videos, contact the following organizations:

Wings for Learning
101 Castleton Street
Pleasantville, NY 10570
Phone 1-800-321-7511
(They sell the 3-2-1 Contact
Rain Forest video, "You
Can't Grow Home Again.")

World Wildlife Fund
1250 24th Street N.W.
Suite 400
Phone 1-202-293-4800
Washington, DC 20037
(They sell a video called
"Rain Forest Rap.")

• Visit a museum, botanical garden, zoo, or aquarium that has a display on rain forests.

• If you visit a rain forest, try not to damage any plants or disturb any animals. Before you take a guided tour, inquire to see how environmentally sensitive the tour company's practices are. Whenever possible, hire local guides and purchase products from local merchants, so local people can benefit from their rain forest park.

• Don't buy endangered rain forest animals or plants or products made from them. If you're in doubt about whether a product is from an endangered animal, or whether it's illegal, don't buy it. The person trying to sell you the product may try to convince you it's okay. For information on what products are okay and what products aren't, write to TRAF-

FIC at the following address and ask for their "Buyer Beware" booklet:

TRAFFIC
World Wildlife Fund
1250 24th Street N.W.
Washington, DC 20037
Phone 1-202-293-4800

• Ask your family to avoid buying furniture and other large products made from tropical rain forest woods such as teak, mahogany, and African walnut.

• You might want to get together a group to do a rain forest fund-raiser. You could hold a bake sale, or sell "Rainforest Crunch" candy, or recycled notepaper and other environmental products. For products you could sell, contact the following:

Community Products, Inc.
R.D. 2
Box 1950
Montpelier, VT 05602
Phone 1-802-229-1840
(They produce "Rainforest Crunch," a product made from nuts sustainably harvested by Amazon natives.)

Real Goods
966 Mazzoni Street
Ukiah, CA 95482-3471
Phone 1-800-762-7325

Seventh Generation
Colchester, VT 05446-1672
Phone 1-800-456-1177

Once you have carried out your fund-raiser, donate your proceeds to an organization that helps protect the rain forest.

One rain forest fund is "Protect an Acre," a program run by the Rainforest Action Network. Money donated to this program is used to help native people protect the rain forests where they live. In the past, money has gone to help Quichua and Shiwiar Indians petition the government of

Ecuador to give them rights to their land. With the help of the fund, the Indians have received rights to 2.5 million acres of forest. For a $25 donation, you will receive a "Protect an Acre" certificate and information on how much land will be saved by the money you donate. Call or write the Rainforest Action Network, listed above, and ask for information on the "Protect an Acre" program.

• Share what you've learned about rain forests with your friends, family, and classmates. You may want to start a campaign to educate people about rain forests— make posters, write an article for the newspaper, and/ or invite speakers on rain forest topics to your school, club, or community center.

• Become pen pals with kids who live in rain forest areas. You can exchange information with them so you'll better understand their lives, their culture and the biome they live in. Within the United States and its territories, Hawaii, Puerto Rico, and the Virgin Islands contain rain forests. Mexico, Belize, Brazil, Costa Rica, and other Neotropical countries contain rain forests, too. For information on becoming a pen pal, write to:

Student Letter Exchange
630 Third Avenue
New York, NY 10017
Phone 1-212-557-3312

• Write letters to state and national government officials, telling them how you feel about rain forest conservation.

• Reduce, reuse, and recycle: the fewer goods you use, the fewer resources have to be used to make them. Some of these resources may be mined or harvested from rain forests.

GLOSSARY

biome an area that has a certain kind of climate and a certain kind of community of plants and animals

buttresses woody supports that grow out from the base of a tree and help bear its weight

canopy the second-highest rain forest layer, formed by the crowns of tall trees. This is the most active layer.

cloud forest rain forest that grows at middle to high elevations, on mountainsides, and is often bathed in clouds and mist; usually cooler, shorter, denser, and mossier than rain forests at lower elevations

consumers animals that cannot make their own food, but must eat plants and/or other animals or fungi

crown the top; leafiest portion of a tree

decomposers organisms that feed on the dead bodies of other organisms, breaking them down into simpler substances

deforestation the destruction of forest by cutting, burning, or other means

emergent tree the tallest trees of the rain forest, which rise up above the forest canopy. They may reach heights of 250 feet (76 meters).

epiphyte a plant that grows on another plant

evapotranspiration the process by which water from inside a plant evaporates over the forest, providing vapor that can form clouds

fragmentation the division of a large portion into smaller pieces

greenhouse effect warming of the earth caused by gases that act like the glass panes of a greenhouse, allowing sunlight into the earth's atmosphere, but only allowing some of the sunlight-generated heat to escape

greenhouse gases gases in the atmosphere that cause the greenhouse effect. These gases keep the earth warm, but lately the quantity of these gases has increased sharply and scientists expect them to cause unfavorable changes in the global climate.

indigenous people people native to a certain area. Often refers to people of the culture who first settled an area.

liana a woody vine that grows up into rain forest trees

Neotropics the tropical areas in North, South, and Central America, plus nearby islands. Also called the American tropics.

plant biomass the weight of all the plant matter—roots, shoots, stems, and other plant parts—for a given area

producers organisms such as plants that make their own food

refugia a place where plants and animals of a biome survived previous ice ages

seed dispersers animals that help to spread seeds

slash-and-burn agriculture ancient type of farming in which people cut down the forest trees and burn the slash—the leftover plant debris—in order to clear the land for growing crops

species diversity the number of different kinds of plants and animals in a given area

sustainable harvest cutting trees, picking crops, or otherwise harvesting resources in such a way that it can be done year after year, indefinitely, without damaging the land

transpiration loss of water through the surfaces of a plant

tropical rain forest natural evergreen forest located in the tropics and characterized by high rainfall

INDEX